THE HOMEWARD PATH

ESSAYS & POETRY

Sara Lee Langsam

AMERISSIS PRESS

Library of Congress Control Number: 2021902103

Langsam, Sara Lee
The Homeward Path / Sara Lee Langsam.
Amerissis Press, 2021
email: langsalight@gmail.com

Trade paperback: 978-0-578-85096-2
Also available in Kindle and Epub versions.

1. God. 2. Universal Power. 3. Faith 4. Poetry 5. Spiritual Path 6. Personal Growth 7. Meditation 8. Religion & Spirituality 9. Spirituality 10. New Age 11. Self-Help 12. Enlightenment I. Title.

Copyright © 2021 by Sara Lee Langsam
Amerissis Press

All rights reserved. No part of this book may be used or reproduced by any means, graphic, electronic, or mechanical, including photocopying, recording, taping, or by any information storage retrieval system without the written permission of the author except in the case of brief quotations in an article or book review.

Printed in the United States of America

Dedication

This book is dedicated to the sons and daughters of God who have walked, are walking, and will walk the Path all the way home.

Acknowledgements

My deepest gratitude goes to my mentors Mark L. Prophet and Elizabeth Clare Prophet for introducing me to the saints who hail from the east and from the west, my dearest friends. Without them, this book would not have been written.

My gratitude also goes to all who helped shepherd my book from concept to publication: Christine Beamer, for helping me begin the process of making the book a reality; my editor Patricia Robertson, for her astute and insightful comments as the book took shape; my book designer Larry Didona, who has been so helpful to me; and finally, Marie Seymour, who shared her deep joy at reading portions of the book and having parts of the book read to her. This gave me the confidence and encouragement to keep on keeping on.

I am so grateful for my family for nurturing me and providing me with the support and acceptance that have been so vital for the fulfilling of my creative potential.

To all my friends who have walked the homeward path with me: I am very grateful for your friendship, comfort, words of wisdom and encouragement.

TABLE OF CONTENTS

ESSAYS

The Homeward Path. 11
What America Means to Me: Freedom of Speech . . 15
The Freedom to Be. 17
Identity 19
Truth and False Truth 23
Integrity 27
The Seen and the Unseen. 31
Kindness 35
Holding on to Your Dreams 37
Maintaining Good Will. 41
Letting Go of Our Memories 45
Gratitude. 49
Do unto Others. 51
Finding Good in Everyone 53
Finding Peace in a World Full of Turmoil. 57

POEMS

YOUR DIVINE PURPOSE

Your Special Tune 61
The Age of Wisdom. 63
The Inner Journey: A Different Kind of Travel 64
The Pearl 66

Origin 68
Atheist 70
Francis Bacon: Prince Tudor 72
Dear Christ Child 74
Christ the Victor 75

CONNECTION TO GOD AND MAN

Connections 79
The Necessary One 81
The Tree of Life 84

OVERCOMING CHALLENGES

My Lovely Forest Rose 87
Climbing a Wall 88
Mountain Climber 89
Overcoming 91
From the Depths 93
Life's Gleanings 94
Pain Is a Teacher 95
The Power of Words 96
Life's Challenges 99
King David's Legacy 100
Finding Peace 102

(Continued on next page)

HELP FROM ON HIGH

Mercy 104
The Cord of Light 105
The Lamb Slain from the Foundation of the World 107
Amethyst Violets 109
The Sprig of Joy. 110

GOD IN NATURE

Lake Loventor. 113
Call of the Sea. 115

IN MEMORIAM: ONE WHO WALKED THE HOMEWARD PATH

Joan: A Servant of God 118

ESSAYS

The Homeward Path

If people would realize that life is a grand design, they would walk with a confident step. We are each born with a specific purpose for our life. Admittedly, it can be hard to discern our purpose.

It may take years to realize and accept that we have a special calling to pursue a certain career, especially when we were trained to do something entirely different. Perhaps it was a lucrative vocation or profession and our family and friends all encouraged us to follow that direction.

One way to ascertain our path is to observe ourselves in many situations and think about what makes us feel especially happy, useful, and confident. These responses are letting us know that this particular activity is very significant in our life scheme.

There is so much extraneous noise in life that it is easy to become distracted and pursue a calling that is not ideal. Only we can know our special purpose. It speaks to us in the quietness of our heart and mind as a still, small voice. It speaks to us as a yearning in our soul that will not let us rest in peace until we pursue it. It manifests as a far-off picture of beauty and peace that we can't quite see clearly and can't quite grasp. It may also manifest as an insistent, demanding voice.

Life may offer us all kinds of treasures: a good job with high pay, a loving family with healthy, happy children, and more. These are all wonderful and should be received in gratitude; yet another important treasure is our special purpose and calling. That special purpose is the gift we have to offer life.

Think of a beautiful wall hanging, a tapestry like the ones from medieval times that hung on castle walls. They were full of scenes from daily life that included a hunt, castle, possibly a beautiful damsel, even a unicorn and many, many flowers. The grand design of our life can be likened to the grand design of a tapestry. This awareness can bring us to a state of awe and wonder as to the meaning of life.

This sense of awe and wonder is a tremendously helpful refuge for us when we are in the midst of a difficult situation. It is easy to lose perspective of who we are and why we are here. Thinking of the tapestry brings us above the stormy seas into the cloudless blue sky—a far better place to be to regain a sense of balance and determination to push on.

Following our life's purpose is an outer and inner journey. The inner journey is subtle and to a great extent we are not aware of it. Yet, as we put all our passion, energy, focus and desire into our life's purpose, the spirit of the Creator grows within us. This is also part of the grand design. Being aware of this, we may proceed with a sense of infinite peace that, in the words of Robert Browning, "God's in His heaven—All's right with the world!"

What America Means to Me: Freedom of Speech

The America in which I grew up was a different place than that which I see around me today. In school and growing up, I always heard it said that people have a right to voice their opinions and the people you defend are those whose opinions are very different from yours. Even those opinions you find abhorrent have the right to be protected. That is the meaning of freedom of speech. It is not necessary to defend someone's freedom of speech if they hold your opinions. There is no need to do so since the opinions are shared and there is total accord.

Nowadays it seems that in many areas of life, there is one point of view that is held up to the public as the only point of view to have. People who hold another point of view are disparaged, scorned and held up to ridicule. Sometimes it is subtle and sometimes it is obvious. It is done with verbal dexterity and often repeated in the media. We also have seen violence or threats of violence used to prevent people from voicing their views.

When there is freedom of speech, everyone has the opportunity to engage in public discourse, voice their opinions, ask their questions and generally learn from one another. This is diversity. Diversity incorporates one's background, education, skills, life experiences and way of being in the world. Diversity brings a richness of different points of view, skills and abilities to the mix. Everyone stands to gain and increase their understanding of the world around them.

There is also a false diversity that is forced on people and leaves one feeling uncomfortable and wrung dry of enthusiasm and sense of security. It is a misuse of power to force people to change their belief systems through ridicule, shaming or threats. We see this happening in our society today.

To be aware of something is to be in a position to handle it and not let it rule you. By our use of free will, we can make decisions that benefit society and ourselves. This is true freedom of speech. We are entering into an era of great possibilities and spiritual freedom. However, there are many dark and discordant elements that oppose and resist this new light. These elements have to be dealt with before we can enter into the joy of a new way of being.

The Freedom to Be

Freedom is the freedom to be. As Shakespeare writes in Hamlet, Act 3 Scene l, "To be, or not to be, that is the question." Being takes great courage and a willingness to persevere against all odds. It means that at some level of being, we realize that there is a purpose, plan or design for everything that is. This purpose is so magnificent that it overwhelms us and we cannot contain it. We can only sense it, acknowledge it and be in awe of it. This awareness can come unexpectedly and unbidden. It can make its presence felt in a mundane, ordinary setting or in a majestic setting, such as a national park, mountain or wilderness area. A good place to experience this is the Grand Tetons.

The memory of this awareness is a special gift granted to us that may last an entire lifetime. Its presence tells us that life holds a great promise that is not always obvious in everyday events. Yet many everyday events hold great promise of joy and hope. A baby stands up for the first time and beams with pleasure, a friend shares a special experience, a loved one smiles in a special way or makes a comment that is so moving it remains with us for a lifetime.

The awareness of being is a gift and a responsibility. Being who we are takes enormous effort, sacrifice and pain. There are dark forces abroad in the world that are bent on the destruction of being. Some of them appear as benign forces and only we know if they are not. We know by the effect they have on us. When we engage them, do they make us feel more or less than who we are or who we want to be? If these forces are not benign, we must never allow them to be arbiters of our destiny.

Being alone for even fifteen minutes is a good place to begin the inner journey. Solitude gives us a certain sense of spaciousness to experience the world. There is the world within and the world without. For us to move in the direction of being who we were designed to be, there must be peace and balance in both worlds. This is what we must strive for. Everything else is a distraction that keeps us focused on an ephemeral goal.

For many of us, there is a sense of hope, faith and expectancy as we pursue our destiny and our willingness to be. Freedom has been designed to help us achieve this worthy purpose.

Identity

One's sense of identity is a force more powerful than many people realize. Our totality of being, our allegiance and willingness to give all our energies to a cause, belief system or vision of life is engaged once we identity with a particular dynamic. That particular dynamic can be based on truth or falsehood. In other words, our sense of identity can make us vulnerable to being used and manipulated by not so benign forces.

During the American Revolutionary War, George Washington had a vision in which a bright angel bearing the American flag said, "Remember, ye are brethren." I ask the reader to keep this in mind as we consider the adage, "In unity is your strength." The truth of this adage is demonstrated in the following Aesop's fable.

An old man had seven sons whom he wanted to imbue with the understanding of the importance of unity. One day he gathered them together to teach them this important lesson. In his hand he held a bundle of sticks securely tied together with strong cord and asked his sons to break the bundle. Each one of them attempted to do so but could not. Then the father untied the cord on the bundle, leaving each stick separate and loose. The brothers had no trouble breaking each individual stick. "'There, my boys,' said he. 'United you will be more than a match for your enemies: but if you quarrel and separate, your weakness will put you at the mercy of those who attack you.'"[1] Thus the father taught his sons the importance of unity, admonishing them never to allow anything in life to disturb their unity of identity as brothers.

What are we to do? Our sense of identity can make us very fragile yet also very strong. It can galvanize us to fight and die for a cause we perceive is of inestimable worth. The sense of a shared identity as Americans is what motivated the founding fathers of our great country to be willing to lay down their lives, their fortunes and their sacred honor to forge a new nation.

What we see today is a distortion and twisting by design of the noble propensity in people to align with the eternal truths—individual freedom, the sacredness of life, and more. What we see is the attempt, often successful, to make "we the people" believe that our identity lies not in the pursuit of truth, of freedom, of honoring the family as the foundation of society, but in our religion, the color of our skin, our nationality, our

---

[1] Aesop's Fables: A New Translation. Father and Sons, trans. V S Vernon Jones. NY: Avenel books, 1988.

gender, our wealth or lack of it and other criteria not of ultimate importance.

What is our identity? What can we identify with that is of supreme value and importance? Every person on earth created by God has the Spirit of the Creator within him or her. It is that Spirit that we all have in common and by which reason we can say we are brethren. With this knowledge we are strengthened.

Therefore, when we encounter the voices of disunity and separation that whisper to us, "You are a this; he is a that; therefore, you are enemies," you will smile. You will say quietly to the malevolent spirit: "This or that will pass away. Today I stand tall in the knowledge that both our identities lie in the Spirit of the Creator within us. We are indeed brethren."

Truth and False Truth

The Miriam-Webster Dictionary defines truth as "the body of real things, events and facts; actuality; the state of being the case."[1] The Wikipedia article on truth states: "Truth is most often used to mean being in accord with fact or reality, or fidelity to an original or standard."[2]

According to these definitions, truth appears to be relatively easy to find in any given situation; but that is not always so. In every area of our society, we are faced with information and facts that are portrayed as true. However, upon closer examination, it turns out that might not be so.

We hear it said that the facts are all in and the conclusion is thus and so. The facts are never all in. Life is an evolutionary process and very often we read in the

---

1   Merriam-Webster Dictionary, s. v. "Truth," (accessed September 23, 2017), https://www.merriam-webster.com/dictionary/truth.

2   Wikipedia, The Free Encyclopedia, s. v. "Truth," (accessed September 23, 2017), https://en.wikipedia.org/wiki/Truth.

media that a former strongly held belief is now being replaced by another conclusion based on evidence that has recently come to light. This is a healthy way to view life. It is not wise or profitable to become attached to one particular way of doing things or viewing the universe.

It is very important to distinguish between eternal verities and relative truth. Eternal verities are truths that never change, such as hope, love, compassion, and conscience. However, relative truth is of an evolutionary nature. It is subject to interpretation and change. This might include different perspectives on how to maintain health of body, mind and emotions.

Some may feel they are following truth and reality. Actually, they are following a relative truth, which is subject to change. This works well if we have all the facts. However, when the facts have been intentionally suppressed or misrepresented, it is almost impossible for us to arrive at a proper conclusion.

How do we know if we are dealing with false truths and how do we proceed? We can assume we are dealing with a false truth if our repeated efforts do not bring about the desired outcome. At this point we must ask ourselves why. Is the information complete? Is it accurate? Are we doing all we can do? We must be willing to look at each component part of the process to see if it will help us reach our goal. If not, we must be willing to change our original premise or move in a different direction.

Life is ongoing and rhythmic and models a swiftly flowing river. We can find harmony, peace and balance if we journey through life pursuing truth in partnership with the eternal verities.

Integrity

The Merriam-Webster Dictionary defines integrity as "firm adherence to a code of especially moral or artistic values: incorruptibility; an unimpaired condition: soundness; the quality or state of being complete or undivided: completeness." This definition is worth considering at length.

Everyone who has written about integrity thinks highly of it as a virtue and lauds the person who has internalized this virtue and lives it in his or her daily life. One prominent Internet blogger states, "It takes having the courage to do the right thing, no matter what the consequences will be."[1] This statement immediately brings to mind Sir Thomas More, Chancellor to Henry VIII and Lord High Chancellor of England from 1529 to 1532. By placing his own conscience above King Henry VIII's demands, Sir Thomas More was tried and convicted of treason and beheaded on July 6, 1535. He told the crowd of spectators that he was dying as the "King's good servant—but God's first."

---

1 Anderson, Amy Rees. "Success Will Come and Go, But Integrity Is Forever", 2012. www.amyreesanderson.com.

Many people recognize the importance of acting and living with integrity in every situation; yet there is also a general awareness that this is extremely difficult to do. A force the size of a tidal wave appears to counter, oppose and overwhelm every laudable action and instance of integrity. This awareness takes us to the word integrity again. What do we see? Embedded in the word "integrity" is the word "grit", which The Merriam-Webster Dictionary defines as "firmness of mind or spirit: unyielding courage in the face of hardship or danger."

It appears that in order to accomplish the task of living with integrity we must also have grit. Integrity can be thought of as our castle—the dwelling place from which we emerge or in which we remain to pursue our daily activities. Grit is the defender of the castle, including the moat, turrets, curtain walls, arrow slits and the fierce army arrayed to fight off all attempted intrusions.

Because integrity is so important for each individual and because it is so difficult to hold on to due to the continual onslaught against it, people who honor integrity and strive to manifest it are often scarred and battle worn. It is neither an easy pursuit nor much admired by many worldly elements. Its adherents are often scorned, reviled, derided, disparaged, defamed and many times destroyed. In spite of these trials and tribulations, many still pursue it with tenacity. This in itself is an act of tremendous courage. These people and their efforts ought to be given the support, praise and acclaim they deserve.

Life, growth, development and maturation are ongoing and continually transforming us. We are not the same person today as we were a year ago, a decade ago, a lifetime ago. Therefore, when we fall short of the mark of perfection in one area or another, we must not treat ourselves harshly. We need to forgive ourselves and try again, remembering that all striving is noble. As has been said, "See everything, overlook a great deal, correct a little." Life is generous and kind and will reward us with the fruit of our labors.

The Seen and the Unseen

We all have an inner guide or compass, which, if we follow its dictates, will lead us unerringly to a wise decision and a positive outcome in any situation. How many times have we met someone and had an immediate response of caution. Something was not quite right. After a bit we got to know them well and felt foolish. We ignored the still small voice within and convinced ourselves they were really all right. Sometime later a series of events occurred that made us wish we had listened to our inner prompting. The still small voice is our conscience—our inner guide. In some religious traditions it is known as our guardian angel. It is sometimes called our higher self. It is always wise to pay heed to its promptings.

In As You Like It, Act 2 Scene 7, Shakespeare wrote: "All the world's a stage, and all the men and women merely players: They have their exits and their entrances; and one man in his time plays many parts, his acts having seven ages." In this light the world can be thought of as a series of scenes where we play the roles assigned to us. The scenes are designed to look a certain way and to make us think about them in a certain way. We need to be very careful and not jump to conclusions nor act in haste. As we make our way carefully through life, the words from 2 Corinthians 4:18 (KJV) come to mind. "While we look not at the things which are seen, but at the things which are not seen: for the things which are seen are temporal; but the things which are not seen are eternal." When we tie ourselves to things that are unseen, we allow entrance into our world the beautiful, the life enhancing, the compassionate and protective spirit of the universe that can sustain us through difficult times.

During difficult times we reexamine all our beliefs and assumptions. Most of the time, we accepted our beliefs when we were young and easily influenced by our family and surroundings. Life was generally good and we had no reason to question what we were taught. During stressful times when things are not going so well, we find ourselves brought up short and in a position to reexamine our deeply held beliefs, values and assumptions. This is not necessarily a bad thing. While this may be considered a crisis, it is also a place and time of great opportunity to decide which of these we want to keep and which ones we can discard. This is a time when we take responsibility for our belief system and accept it as part of our conscious identity.

Our greatest aid and ally in this enormous endeavor is our ever-present yet unseen higher self. The higher self is a link to the eternal essence of ultimate wisdom to which we have access. Our great need is our goad to pursue this inner wisdom and courage. How do we begin? We can journal. We can take walks in nature or any beautiful setting. We can listen to our favorite music. We can choose whatever gives us a sense of peace, beauty and comfort. We have begun a journey that will be a source of joy, peace and illumination for us and lead us on to ever expanding horizons.

Kindness

When we look for the definition and description of kindness, we see that kindness is a behavior marked by ethical characteristics, a pleasant disposition and concern for others. In Rhetoric, Aristotle defines it as being "helpfulness towards someone in need, not in return for anything, nor for the advantage of the helper himself, but for that of the person helped."[1]

The importance of kindness and the benign and lasting effect it has on the recipient is often overlooked in the turbulence of the fray, which oft times characterizes the daily life experience of many. Too often we are so engaged in the minute-by-minute struggle of our everyday lives that we hang on tightly to the trees and fail to see the beauty and interconnectedness of the forest.

It is only when we are overtaken by a sudden unexpected dire turn of events that we begin to understand how vulnerable and needy we truly are and to be grateful for the salve that is gently applied to our open

---

1 Aristotle, Rhetoric, trans. W. Rhys Roberts (Internet Classics Archive, n.d.), bk. 2, http://classics.mit.edu/Aristotle/rhetoric.2.ii.html.

wounds. That salve is the soothing balm of kindness administered by one who may be a dear friend, a loved one, or a complete stranger. In that moment, we understand the importance of administering kindness with the warmth of an open heart that seeks only to allay suffering and distress with no thought of personal gain. The blessings of the universe gently enfold both the giver and the receiver of an act of kindness.

Holding on to Your Dreams

Our dreams are our lease on life. They give us the hope, joy, and faith to hold on through difficult times. When we falter and fall, we have the strength to pick ourselves up and start all over again because of our dreams. We must never loose our hold on our dreams but have a sense of patience and overcoming—a confidence and belief in our victory. No matter how dark the landscape appears, no matter how bleak the prospects, we retain the sense of ultimate victory. This is a distinct possibility to accomplish and has been achieved by many people.

In order to have dreams in the first place, we need to be able to envision them. Holding onto a vision of exactly what we want to manifest is vitally important to nourish our aspirations. The more detailed and clear our vision, the more likely that we will get exactly what we want.

Many years ago, I saw before my inner vision a beautiful large garden and expansive backyard easily seen from glass doors in a large house. The scene would come back to me many times and it would nurture my sense of wellbeing. It was only a few years ago, thinking back on my life, when I realized that I actually did live in a house with a view almost exactly like the one I had envisioned years before.

Some people have actually made a scrapbook of pictures that depict their ideal future. They have cut out pictures of houses, rooms and landscapes, even men or women who looked like the type of person they would like to marry. For many of them it worked and they got exactly what they had put into the scrapbook. The more realistic and exact we can make the visualization or find a likeness in a picture, the greater the probability it will materialize.

The same is true of feeling drawn to a particular career or vocation. Many children have a strong sense of what they want to do and what career they want to pursue. Encouraging a child to watch and ask questions of a person in a particular vocation is very helpful as they decide whether or not to pursue that path. It is never a waste of time to pursue an interest in one vocation or career since life is so different today and faster paced than it was even several decades ago. Even if a vocation appears not to be accessible to a child for one reason or another, they still will have gained a lot. The child or adult can pursue it as an avocation or hobby.

The more interests and skills individuals cultivate

throughout their lives, the more enriched their lives will be. It is a wonderful gift to surround ourselves with the people and interests that give us pleasure. Our dreams form the structure of our lives.

Maintaining Good Will

The spiritual-material universe was created by a benign force known to many as Deity, God, Father of Lights, Father and more. Our Creator harbors only good will toward His creation. The entire spirit-matter universe is designed to be a reservoir of light, love, abundance and nurture, causing the myriad creation to flourish and increase. Therefore, it behooves us who are a part of the creation to look upon all that surrounds us with good will. As we are God's offspring, we may appropriate the Father's good will to ourselves and to others as we interact with one another in our daily affairs.

Why maintain good will? The set of the sail determines the outcome of the voyage. Good will is holding a positive attitude toward every individual, circumstance and situation. It is a strong desire to see everyone fulfill the cosmic purpose for which he or she was created. The powerful intention and the overwhelming love of the universe acts as a magnet to draw to each individual the exact vibration, positive and negative, that the individual has sent forth. Therefore, an individual who consistently holds every person and situation with positive regard, and desires only the best outcome for all, will at some point in his or her life reap a bountiful harvest of blessings. I have seen this law operate in my life and in the lives of those around me.

Many will exclaim as they read these words that the writer is advocating an excessively optimistic attitude, an attitude that is unrealistic because of the many situations and individuals that do not have benign tendencies and elements within them. That is why good intentions and great love are not enough. We need to add to our quiver of arrows great wisdom and the ability to discern the truth in every situation.

A story comes to mind—a tale from ancient China. A poor peasant and his wife were blessed with a baby son. Their neighbors celebrated the couple's good fortune in having a son who would be a mainstay in old age. Time went by and when the boy was a young lad, someone gave him a horse as a gift. Again the neighbors rejoiced in the lad's good fortune in receiving such a fine animal. One day as the boy was riding the horse, the horse tripped and threw the boy off its back. The lad suffered a broken leg that didn't heal properly and left him disabled with a limp. The neighbors exclaimed how unfortunate the parents were to have a crippled son who would never be able to make a good marriage.

Sometime after that incident, a nearby country

attacked the kingdom. The emperor sent his officials to all the villages of China to pick out young men for his army. These officials eventually came to the village where the peasant, his wife and their son lived. The officials scrutinized every young man carefully and took those of a certain age in good physical condition. The villagers were saddened because now there was no one to help with the planting and harvesting of crops. Many young men who had been conscripted would likely never make it home. The peasant's son, however, was not chosen for the emperor's army. Once again, the peasant's neighbors exclaimed how fortunate the peasant was because his son was disabled.

This simple story holds a great truth. Sometimes it is not evident whether or not an occurrence is fortunate or unfortunate. Only time will tell. We need to look to truth as our ally and wisdom as our comfort as we navigate the currents of life.

Letting Go of Our Memories

Memories, especially good memories, are pillars of comfort that sustain us in times of trial. Just as we lean against a pillar when we cannot stand alone without undue exertion, so memories support us to maintain a confident, cheerful attitude. Sometimes, however, memories can be painful and difficult. They can be like a sharp piece of metal that we try to avoid stepping on at all costs. Sometimes these memories sit quietly in our subconscious, so quietly that we do not even know they are there. However, they give off an unpleasant and untraceable odor that influences our thoughts and behavior without our realizing why we think and act in a particular way.

A consistent pattern of negativity that is not tied in any way to the present situation usually has its origin in a past memory or a painful incident. It is actually fun to be a sleuth and see if we can follow the string of thoughts and feelings to their origin. Sometimes we have an aha moment and make the connection. Sometimes the pattern is elusive, slipping in and out among the bulrushes in the swamp and refuses to be caught. At this point we need to let it go and go back to our daily occupations until another opportunity presents itself.

There is a third kind of memory that presents itself as positive and comforting. This is usually a memory of an activity we engaged in either by ourselves or with others that was fun and full of enjoyment. This type of memory can be a barrier to moving onto other experiences. We become attached to the memory because to leave it will create a vacuum and this we are hesitant to do. Sometimes we have to be willing to leave the familiar for the unknown just as Christopher Columbus left Spain for an unknown land. He had to risk the unknown in order to find a land, America, which would be greatly loved, by those who also had to leave what they knew well in order to find a better place. As the poem by Emma Lazarus says, "Give me your poor, your tired, your huddled masses yearning to breathe free..."

The key words here are uncertainty, risk, hope and freedom. For the hope of a freer life, many people have endured risk and uncertainty. We must never forget that the promise of freedom has called millions to our shores to pursue a life of hard work sustained by their dreams of a better life for themselves and their progeny.

We, too, must take that risk if we are to breathe free in our own newly found land of freedom and opportunity. We must let go of the hand of the known and venture out into the unknown in order to fulfill our cosmic destiny.

Gratitude

Gratitude acts as a balm to the one who sends it forth as well as to the one who receives it. The balm spreads itself over the entire consciousness, being and world of the recipient and the sender as a healing unguent, enveloping each one's particular outlook on life with a healing and soothing effect. No matter what has gone before or what will come after, the moment of gratitude is a time of blessing and renewal. We can think of a stone cast into a lake causing a series of ever-expanding ripples.

When we feel and express gratitude about anything large or small, we are creating a magnet that will in due course return to us more of the same. This is a universal law and we can experiment with it as we please. We have nothing to lose and much to gain.

Many people take much of what they have for granted. They don't feel gratitude because they can't imagine life being any different. This is not so much a lack of gratitude as a lack of experience and a perspective that fails to take into account the many possibilities that life may present to us. At some point in life, we realize that what we take for granted is something many others have not experienced and therefore have a great yearning for that particular element of life.

At times our perspective is expanded when we lose what we have taken for granted through some misfortune. Now, we can look back and realize that some aspect of life that we assumed was ours is now denied to us. Although this is a very difficult and painful process, it also brings with it a greater awareness of the vicissitudes of life and helps us appreciate what we do have. If we use this growing awareness as an opportunity to be grateful for everything we have, especially what we may have overlooked in the past, then we are creating a strong magnet to bring into our lives more for which to be grateful. Gratitude is a way of life that never stops giving. It is the oil that smooths over the rougher parts of the road we must travel.

Do Unto Others

The golden rule of doing unto others as we would have others do unto us is well known to almost everyone. We can alter it just a bit and get a more serious statement: As you do unto others, so shall it be done unto you. This statement brings to mind two long-held adages. One comes directly from Jesus: "As ye give so shall ye receive." The other is common wisdom: "What goes around comes around."

The potential meaning is quite interesting and deserves a period of unhurried contemplation. What can this mean? In my essay on gratitude, we read, "When we feel and express gratitude about anything large or small, we are creating a magnet that will in due course return to us more of the same. This is a universal law and we can experiment with it as we please." Is this law an example of "like attracts like"? It appears that there is a magnetic impulse in the universe that identifies many types of energetic responses and returns each response to its owner such that "like attracts like" or "birds of a feather flock together."

When we have learned this universal principle, we can use it to our advantage and are thereby empowered to have greater dominion over our life. What a blessing to each one from the universe. As we add gratitude to our knowledge and use of the law, we are multiplying and strengthening the good that will return to us through our wise choices.

Finding Good in Everyone

It is generally believed by most people that we are the handiwork of the Creator. In Genesis 1:31 (KJV) we read, "God saw all he had made, and indeed it was very good." Once we accept this statement, we realize that this applies to everyone we meet along the path of life regardless of their outer appearance. Therefore, it is incumbent upon each of us who believes in and lives by the word of our Creator to immediately look for and focus upon the good we see in every individual we meet.

Why is this so difficult to do? There are several reasons. First of all, many people are not aware of these words. They may never have read them or if they have, it was a long time ago and they have relegated them to a distant part of their conscious awareness. Secondly, we live in a world where criticism is rife and most people are used to being the recipient of some sort of criticism. We would be wise to soothe our injuries with the balm of gentleness and compassion. We might also want to place this balm on those who have inflicted the wounds upon us. Healing their wounds will redound to our advantage in that they will not have as great a need to inflict pain on others.

When we find good qualities in someone we meet and act in a positive way toward them, we are applying the balm of gratitude and good will and this will have good consequences. To focus on and feel appreciation for a particular quality is to enhance and magnify that quality. Interestingly enough, the same holds true for negative qualities. All adults who interact with children need to be very careful how they approach the subject of behavior. It is far more constructive to let a child know how proud you are of them for a particular behavior they exhibited than to angrily accuse them of some negative behavior they may also have demonstrated.

In general, children want and need the love and approval of the adults around them. A kind and complimentary word will work wonders with a child and an adult as well. Another reason it is so difficult to find the good in everyone is that some people keep the good part of themselves very well hidden. They are too busy demonstrating the not so good part of themselves. If we are determined to follow the admonition to find the good in everyone, it behooves us to persist until we find it. That may take time, effort and patience. However, it is well worth the effort, for a soul burdened with great darkness has been liberated. Life will surely provide us with many opportunities to hone our skills in this endeavor.

Finding Peace in a World of Turmoil

Nowadays it is difficult to find a peaceful moment. Peace, a great blessing that is often overlooked or taken for granted, needs to be absorbed. Its quiet comfort, its serene outpicturing, acts as a balm that enters our every pore and cell. Once inside us, it fills all spaces and allows us to see life from a different perspective. Life is in a constant flow. When we attune ourselves with life, we go with the flow. Each one sees life with a different perspective and makes contact with life's originator in a unique way.

When peace eludes us, it is often because the peaceful moment is not forthcoming. At the present moment there is much turbulence, turmoil and activity that seeks to catch and engage our energies. Social media and the general media are a great draw on our attention. They don't allow us to curl up with a book in our favorite chair or space where we are in control of the situation, where we are free to read, think about what we are reading, think about what we want to think about, or not think at all.

Social media is interactive and the media in general has its own agenda. The individuals involved know how to elicit and draw forth from the reader or viewer certain powerful responses. These can create a disturbing or unpleasant sensation within that is not conducive to a peaceful experience.

What can we do to protect ourselves? We have a right to find a moment of peace on a regular basis. We all have our own inner knowing of what makes us feel peaceful. For some it is listening to beautiful music or looking at or being in a beautiful natural setting. For others it is being alone or with a person with whom they have a deep connection. It is a healing experience to decide what makes us feel peaceful and pursue it. Peace is the anchor point of being. It is greatly to be treasured and worth whatever it takes to achieve it.

POEMS

YOUR DIVINE PURPOSE

Your Special Tune

Every child is special
With a certain role to play.
When you were born you heard a song,
A tune that led the way.

It called to you to come apart
And listen deep within.
You have a gift of hope and joy
To share with everyone.

This gift can be a smile
That always lights your face.
Your friends are glad to share your joy.
Each has a special place.

Always listen to your song.
Its tune is just for you.
Within your heart the words impart
A message clear and true.

They tell you how to bring your gift
To places far and wide.
Some people you may never see.
Some will be at your side.

What matters is the light you spread
Will lighten people's way.
Clouds of gloom will disappear
And leave a perfect day.

The Age of Wisdom

Close your eyes and you will go
To a place where soft winds blow,
Where joy and hope and gratitude
Are the soul's daily food.

Where every day and hour is spent
In fruitful endeavor and serious intent,
Where holy purpose does impart
A coil of Light from the heart
Forming a ladder of rectitude
To be used for mankind's good.

Each rung an opportunity
For wisdom gained and mastery
That civilization might secure
For every noble heart and pure
The purpose towards which it does aspire,
Which is to rise higher and higher
Until at last its vision won
The tiny flame is now a Sun.
Each Ray of Light is now a part
Of God the Father's sacred heart.

The Inner Journey: A Different Kind of Travel

Riding on a train, our face pressed against the window,
We observe the landscape as it appears, then fades into
    the distance.

The blue sky is a backdrop for a constantly changing
    panorama of urban and rural scenes:
Streets, houses, billboards, empty factories, shopping
    malls
Now set in a more pastoral landscape.

Gardens, streams, farms, horses grazing, forests, wide
    spaces greet our eyes.

The soul is satisfied with this visual feast.
She relaxes.
She is ready for the inner journey.
The Presence presides over the inner journey.
Love and wisdom are there to tutor the soul
And guide her along the pathways of Life.

Each step taken leads the soul closer to a place of
 beauty and peace
That is greater than what she has known before.
She can take this gift and apply it to the vicissitudes of
 life.
The inner journey has made the outer journey richer
 and more meaningful.
Both journeys are important for the well-lived life.

The Pearl

I gazed into the sea one day
At the break of dawn.
Golden rays were flooding the sky,
A bright new day was born.

Lo before my very eyes
A wondrous pearl appeared.
Its whiteness showed, its brightness glowed
Its magnificence I revered.

In purity it spoke to me
Of splendor I might see,
Were I to look within my heart
With pure humility,
Where reigns Lord Christ that noble knight
To him we bend the knee.

The soul who kneels to her liege Lord
Is raised triumphantly.
In love amending every wrong,
In temptation being tried,
The soul as victor wears the crown
And sits at Christ's right side.

Gratefully did I behold
That wondrous orb so white,
Which gently taught my striving soul
To wear a robe of Light.

Origin

Part One: In the Beginning

Lightning flashes forth,
Light descends in waves.
Myriad seeds of Light seed the mighty cosmos.

It is the Father's will.
His offspring, heirs apparent, now fill his universe.
Galaxies, star systems, systems of worlds, planets—
All home to his beloved, his sons and daughters.

This is our identity to claim.
We carry the spark of divinity within ourselves—
A spark that knows its origin,
A magnet that unerringly seeks its source.

Part Two: Maya

Maya is illusion.
Do not be led astray by illusion.
Remember our Source.
Our Source is infinite.
Our Source is within.
Our finite selves house an infinite seed.

One day this seed will return to its Source.
It can do naught else.
It is destined to become one with the All One,
To return to the wave of Light
From which it descended.

Our destiny is written in the stars.
Maya, illusion, will vanish away and be no more.
Reality will be apparent to the beloved of God's heart.
His progeny will seed the universe.

Atheist

Lord God of Hosts
How wondrous is thy name in all creation.
The universes, galaxies, solar systems and planets
All sing thy praise as they move to the sound of the
    Om.

The majestic Hum.
The Hum of Eternity, the Hum of Infinity,
The Hum of the Soundless Sound.

We your children are heirs to the promise
That one day we will inherit all that you are.
Our royal robes of purple
Will flow with the Wave of Light
As it spans the Spirit-Matter Universe.

This is the inheritance, the destiny and the grandeur
That the atheist renounces.
You may use your free will
To deprive yourself of the vision of splendor.

Having squeezed your consciousness
Into a limited, constricted mold,
It has suffered the ignominy of deformity
And grown accustomed to this spiritual handicap.

Be of good cheer.
You are not doomed to remain
A servant of this blighted state.

Kuan Yin, the Goddess of Mercy,
Extends her arms to you
In limitless compassion
To heal your unfortunate condition
And return you to your original state—
A child of the Most High God
Whose inheritance is to sing with the stars
In a realm of Glory.

Dedicated to all atheists.
Like the prodigal son,
May you return to the loving embrace
Of our Father-Mother God.

Francis Bacon: Prince Tudor

Dream on young lad,
The world's your stage.
Dream bold, dream far, dream free.
What suits you lad?
What makes you glow?
What guides you faultlessly?

You were born with a special plan,
A blueprint for your life.
From early youth you had a goal,
A vision that you kept.
The whole wide world was your domain
To help mankind accept
That each one has a destiny,
Each has a solid worth,
To leave the world a better place
Than when it gave him birth.

You labor long, you labor hard,
You give your very all.
You'll leave the earth a better place
Where people can stand tall.

Their knowledge, their ideas,
The very words they speak
Have the power to convey deep thoughts
To reach the haughty and the meek.

What comes forth from your pen
As tiny seeds of Light
Will take root around the world
Will cause error to take flight.

The universe is man's domain,
His spirit can run free.
In partnership with all of Life
Is Man's great destiny.

Dear Christ Child

Dear Christ Child of Bethlehem
Asleep within my heart.
The tender ray of mercy's love
You shall to life impart.

The glory we shall one day be—
Heir to God's throne divine.
When we together all life raise
The Real Self reign sublime.

Christ the Victor

O let us slay the carnal mind
That slays the good in all.
When one foot forward we would put,
The not-self makes us fall.

Until we bend the knee to Christ,
The Light that lights us all,
And claim the victory of Right,
As Victor we stand tall.

POEMS

CONNECTION TO GOD AND MAN

Connections

We are all connected.
Somewhere, some place
You and I have held a space
That kept us connected
As friend, loved one, adversary, foe.
These ties bind us wherever we go.

Whenever we meet we sing a song.
A tune that plays on all day long.
Beautiful melody, haunting refrain
Brings us together again and again.

To increase the good we were wont to do,
To erase the stain made before we knew
About Life's purpose—Life's great plan
To raise us higher so our eyes can span
The vision of the ages as vistas unfold.
We were created out of a perfect mold.

Time and space both play their part
To help create a work of art.
That work is man and woman too.
We decide what we shall do.
To live our lives with Virtue and Grace
Erase all stain and hold our place.

We are pillars in the Temple of Truth
As we unite to teach our youth.
God's great dream—the Brotherhood of Man
All work together to fulfill God's plan.
Outward differences, discord and strife
Fade away, disappear—it is God's life.

Truth says, sons and daughters, behold!
Ye are all created in the perfect mold.
Reach for your future, it beckons you.
Release your grip on the lesser view.
Keep your eye on the goal and you shall see
A mighty victory for you and me.

The Necessary One

Each one is essential,
Part of the whole.
We each have a talent
Our gift to bestow
Upon the needy,
The sick and infirm,
The hopeless, the desolate,
The injured who yearn
For a better tomorrow
When the sun will shine.
They will rise to their fullness
Greet their destiny sublime.

We all are the needy,
The sick and infirm.
Though we seem strong and able
We have lessons to learn.

From all we encounter,
From those far and near,
Their ideas, their vision,
Their purpose is clear.

Look not to another
To make the wheel turn.
It is your strength, your effort,
Your faith that will earn
Renewed opportunity
For all to partake
In earth's great future.
An Age is at stake.

The Age of Aquarius,
Whose dawn does unfold,
Promises Peace and Brotherhood—
These will take hold.

Together we span
A tapestry of Light.
Together we win
The glorious fight.
Expansive, unfolding,
The Light does descend.
True to God's wishes
We will win in the end.

The Tree of Life

I gaze upon the Tree of Life
Its towering branches spread far and wide.
Beneath its shade all dwell in peace,
In joy and fullness all abide.

All who hunger need but look
Upon a green and leafy bough,
And pluck a fruit that they might eat,
With life's abundance be endowed.

All who falter along life's way,
Whom cares and burdens cause to fall,
Can rest beneath the dappled leaves,
And be renewed to strive once more.

Each of us is a Tree of Life
To those who nestle 'neath our wings,
The comfort that we in love impart
Does cause the weary heart to sing.

POEMS

OVERCOMING CHALLENGES

My Lovely Forest Rose

It was a lovely summer's day,
The air was bright and clear.
I strode abroad in search of Truth
And Beauty drew me near.

Into the forest I did walk.
My sword hung at my side,
Lest fate decree maliciously
My destiny be denied.

I was aware as I set forth
Into that wild domain
That shadows lurked
And snares were set
To cause me grief and pain.

The Purity that I did seek,
The Truth and Beauty dear,
To me were hidden
Till I should prove
My victory over fear.

Climbing A Wall

A high, smooth stone wall—
I am climbing this wall.
Each step is excruciatingly difficult.
It takes all of my effort and energy.
I am laboring under the burden.
God is giving me the will to go on.
The blue sky is above.
Even though I am not looking at it,
Its presence is felt at deep levels.

Mountain Climber

I yearn to reach the mountaintop,
To climb and climb and never stop.
I feel the sun and see the sky.
My soul soars like a bird on high.
My soul soars high, my thoughts roam free.
To be pure light is my destiny.

The climb is long and hard and slow.
I must decide which way to go.
The easy way is not to be.
Its false smile beckons me.
Without a pause I journey on
To forge ahead to strive beyond.

Though my feet are on the ground,
My heart in hope and love abounds,
In faith that one day I will reach the summit,
Will touch the sky.
My feet will no more be confined
To a rocky path, to fall behind.

Every step carries me home
Where loved ones from all ages join
In heartfelt prayer that we'll soon be
Together for all eternity.

Overcoming

Wherever I go, whatever I do
From the shadows, from behind the door
Out pops you!

You can be a scary thought.
I want to run and hide.
The more I want to change my space
You're always at my side.

I tell myself to wait awhile.
The landscape will dissolve.
We'll see things in a different light.
Difficulties will resolve.

The new day dawns.
It gives me hope.
We're on the homeward path.
We still face challenges supreme
And beings full of wrath.

We must stand fast no matter what
Until the wrath subsides.
The fear that sits upon our chest
Will not prevent our stride.

With determination and a prayer
We continue on our way.
Sunlight shines upon our face.
We greet the bright new day.

From the Depths

Obstacles, difficulties, uncertainties, dangers
Arise from the depths.
The path to the underworld
Is narrow and formidable.
We need balance
To remain steady on our feet.

There is nothing to hold onto
But inner guidance and bearing.
The signposts are marked.
They are within ourselves.

To make the determination
Not to move forward is wise.
Better to wait for the inner strength,
Fortitude and steadiness we need
To enter the Wild Land.

Life's Gleanings

Pain exists.
It is absorbed.
Its elements are used
To create a tensile structure
Of strength and endurance.

Rods of light
Are used to uphold
An edifice of wisdom
Whose spires reach
Into infinity.

Pain Is a Teacher

Pain is a teacher.
It is teaching me something.
I listen patiently no longer feeling fear,
No longer feeling imprisoned.
My acceptance and willingness to listen
Creates space for me to be, to grow, to become.
I enter, absorb and flow
Into a large, beautiful space
Of infinite possibilities.
My willingness to accept and adapt
Has transformed my reality
Into a realm of peace.

The Power of Words

Words are powerful.
Each word is a chalice or cup.
It holds light.
It bestows light on those who receive it.

The Word can heal.
The Word can comfort.
The Word can enlighten.
The Word can bless.

Words are tiny cups of light
Holding together the Spirit-Matter Cosmos.

Each word bestowed in love is a blessing to all who are touched by it.
One word can cause a chain reaction
That passes light from one person to another
Blessing each one.

The Word is the light of Cosmos.
Let us give adoration to the Word.

And then the dark ones came.
The Word in all its glory and power
Was usurped by the brothers of the shadow
Who took the precious cup of light, of comfort,
Of healing, of enlightenment, of blessing
And into the chalice poured venom, poured discord,
Poured darkness of all sorts.

Thus began the woes of humanity.
Thus began strife, discord, enmity and pain.

The Word in all its power
Acts at all levels and sub levels of being.
The dark ones used the Word as a weapon
To undermine the sense of wellbeing of the soul.

The innocent soul
Wearing its coat of many colors
Finds its coat is stained
By the misused Word
Causing fear, shame, guilt, anxiety, despair.

The soul cries out for help.
The Good Physician cometh
Bringing healing in his wings.
The Good Physician brings the Cup of Light,
The Word that can override the darkness.

Let us kneel in supplication and gratitude
Before the Good Physician,
Christos, the Logos, the Word.

Life's Challenges

When the going gets rough as it sometimes does,
The impulse is strong to get up and move,
To vacate and leave the difficult scene
And go to a place far more serene.

The courage it takes to remain in one spot,
To face and endure your challenging lot,
That courage will find you alone in the end
All one with the I AM
Your magnificent friend.

King David's Legacy

Our beloved Samuel,
Israel's prophet of long ago,
Anointed a king at God's command,
A shepherd boy to rule the land.

David, a lad of beauty and grace,
With courage beheld the enemy's face.
His love of God and trust in him
Allowed him a mighty victory to win.

For although before him stood
A giant of seeming magnitude,
His piercing eye and forceful blow
Caught the enemy and laid him low.

When we find ourselves oppressed
By grievous sorrows upon our breast,
Let us hearken back to days of yore
That by Life's joy we be restored.

Let gentle wisdom be our guide
Until all gloom and darkness subside,
As we stand fast our heads held high
In honor to fulfill our destiny.

Finding Peace

A peaceful moment.
A necessity we treat as a luxury.
So difficult to find.
So difficult to hold onto.
A great blessing yet often overlooked or taken for granted.
Peace—a quiet comfort.
Its balm enters us and pours into every cell.

Its presence allows us to attune with the flow of life.
Where can we find peace?
We find peace when we bathe our eyes in beauty.
The beauty of nature.
The beauty of stillness.
The beauty of solitude.

Peace—the anchor point of being.
A priceless treasure, a holy experience.
A connection to higher worlds.
All is well.
Amen.

POEMS

HELP FROM ON HIGH

Mercy

Mercy is a drop of rain
Upon a parched flower,
A rainbow of promise
To a weary traveler,
Sunlight warming
A shivering child,
A fragrant breeze
In a meadow.

Mercy is found in the heart
Of one who takes the time
To listen to a tale of woe
And extends the hand of comfort
To ease the pain.

The Cord of Light

The lifeline of poetry
Drops from the sky
I hold on tightly
It raises me high.

Pictures of beauty
Whose stories unfold
Keep my gaze resting
On a pure lovely mold.

Patterns of beauty
Of joy and of peace
Release me from sadness
All sense of dis-ease.

My soul is united
With beauty and grace
I am lifted on high
To a wonderful place.

I am nourished and fed
On droplets of light
A cradle of innocence
Whose strands woven tight
Provide a safe haven
Keep out the dark night.

My soul is protected
Is safe and secure
"All is well," say the angels.
"You need suffer no more."

The Lamb Slain from the Foundation of the World

The sheep know the voice of the Good Shepherd.
The Good Shepherd leads the flock beside the cool waters
That they may drink and be refreshed and renewed.
Their throats are parched and dry.
They have wandered in the wilderness for a long time
Hungering after Truth and Righteousness,
Neither of which have they received from the false shepherds,
Who have smiled and offered empty words of comfort
When within they are ravening wolves
Who seek only their own power, their own selfish ends, their own fortunes.

The Good Shepherd loves the sheep.
He gives his life for his sheep,
Accepting abuse, vilification, and threats
From those whom he has replaced.
The sheep know the voice of the Good Shepherd.

They know his deep commitment, his love.
He bears their burdens,
Carrying those who can go no farther in his arms and on his back.
The light from his blood is offered as sustenance to the helpless sheep.
He gives them hope, strength and renewed determination to press on.

Throughout history on our planet
In times of great crisis and need
There has appeared the Good Shepherd—the Lamb.
Let us pause and give gratitude for the Good Shepherd,
The Lamb slain from the foundation of the world.

Amethyst Violets

Amethyst violets
Droplets afire.
Cool to my fingertips
My love you inspire.

Each droplet a virtue,
Mercy's at hand,
Amethyst violets
Now cover the land.

The Sprig of Joy

The Sprig of Joy eternally
Brings blessings of good cheer
To all who seek it in good faith,
To all who venture near.

The tiny leaves so dewy green,
Flowers of rosy pink,
Cause hearts to sing in gratitude
And on good thoughts to think.

The song is carried on the wind,
Its wings of joy to spread.
Each thought of love so crystal pure
Flies to each willing head.

POEMS

GOD IN NATURE

Lake Loventor

PART ONE: DAWN

In a tiny forest in a faraway place,
Hidden among the leafy trees,
Surrounded by an air of heavenly peace,
Lies Lake Loventor calm and serene,
Radiating beauty to all who are near.

Her calm waters tinted with the coming dawn,
Silver grey, light yellow and rosy pink,
Saying that night is gone, a new day is born.
Still is the air with a hushed reverence
In this everlasting moment of majestic beauty.

PART TWO: AT NOON

Lies Lake Loventor calm and serene,
Golden fire upon her waters,
Sparkling diamonds dancing the waves,
Reflecting the brilliance of the noonday sun.
A moment of exquisite golden beauty.

Part Three: At Night

Glows the bright amber moon o'er the calm lucid
    water,
Reflecting its light on the rippling waves.
The leaves on the trees sway ever so gently,
Lightly in rhythm with the cool summer breeze.

Quietly lie her azure waters
Dozing beneath a star-sprinkled sky.
Soft are the sighs of the tiny ripples.
Still are the sounds in the forest beyond.

The night has enveloped the world in its covers.
It lies undisturbed in repose.

Call of the Sea

Sharp is the sting of the gusty wind
As it smacks against my face.
Sharp is its sting on the wings of a gull
As it soars through the vast blue space.

Warm are the golden rays of the sun
Drenching, engulfing me.
Warm as the blood in my restless heart
That throbs to the mood of the sea.

Soft are the hues of the waking sun
Blending with foamy spray.
But loud and urgent the call of my soul
That only the sea can allay

IN MEMORIAM:

One Who Walked the Homeward Path

Joan: A Servant of God

A life lived in pursuit of a dream.
A life lived in pursuit of wholeness.
A soft voice, a gentle demeanor
Covered a white-hot intensity and steely determination.
She looked to community as a nurturing presence—
A mother drawing her children to her.

Joan traveled far and wide,
Her free spirit searching for wholeness, resolution,
Enlightenment and peace.
She traversed the world—
No boundaries or restrictions
Would she accept in her life.
Always searching, growing and overcoming,
Being patient when the situation required,
Yet filled with hope for a better tomorrow.

Joan was one who knew that her destiny was to reach the stars.
She lived her life with a fiery, steely, unwavering determination
To arrive at the goal having made all things right.
Now she has found the comforting embrace of her Presence.

Afterword

Those who have experienced editing a manuscript come to understand that it can always be refined. At one point we say, "I choose to stop here. Life is a transcendent experience. There is never a real end."

Biography

Sara Lee Langsam taught high school Spanish and English as a Second Language in high school and elementary school. Words have always fascinated her and the beauty and meaning of life that can be captured in poetry.

She has written three books of poetry: *Angels and Fairies and Bright Rainbows,* (original edition), *Angels and Fairies and Bright Rainbows* (expanded edition), and *The Voice of the Heart.* She also has published two children's books—*Francis Bacon: England's True Prince* and *Francis and Anthony: Inseparable Brothers.* Her most recent book, *The Homeward Path,* includes both poems and essays.

Sara Lee's poems, essays, and children's stories portray on a subtle level the ideas and concepts she has learned in her lifetime of studying the world's many spiritual and religious traditions. The knowledge of these traditions and their role in our everyday life has given the author the opportunity through her books to share with others these vital life-enhancing concepts.

www.ingramcontent.com/pod-product-compliance
Lightning Source LLC
LaVergne TN
LVHW051135080426
835510LV00018B/2421